This book is incre[illegible] used by business leaders, executive[illegible] leadership manual for all businesses [illegible]nals.

The use of comp[illegible] and governance jargon has been [illegible]nd it to be quite captivating with great intellectual stimulation that is underpinned by its unique flair of simplicity that embodies the authors' wealth of knowledge and experience.

Chaka Nkofo CD(SA),
Chief Executive, Institute of Directors Lesotho

The reason that this book is so superb is that it is based around a very simple concept. If you want a book about academic theory, look elsewhere. The advice is blunt, practical and often entertaining. Read this book and you will feel a great deal more comfortable in the pilot seat of your own company.

Graham Davies

This is a great book for anyone in business – whatever its size and whatever shape it's in. It's written in a compellingly simple, easy-to-follow way while focusing your mind on the areas which will determine whether your business booms or busts.

Michael Dodd

This book is the best comprehendible book for painting the whole picture of business – so providing it to managers helps me to move many of them forward more swiftly.

Doug Bannister, Chief Executive, The Port of Dover

I spent some years working closely with the CEO of a major bank and during this time I spent a fabulous year at MIT's Sloan School – and duly had my head filled with just about everything. Problem is, it has taken me all this time to actually pull it together and make the school stuff coherent – and it is the book *Staying in the Helicopter®* that has done that.

Paul Clark, Paul Clark & Associates

STAYING IN THE HELICOPTER®

The key to sustained profitable growth

ROGER HARROP
JUANITA VORSTER

Publisher: The CEO Experts™
Website: www.theceoexperts.com

1st Edition authored by Roger Harrop, published in in 2005 by LeHeup 1000 Ltd (ISBN 0-954958-60-8)
Revised edition published in 2006 by LeHeup 1000 Limited.
Reprinted 2008, 2009, 2011 , 2013, 2016, 2018.
Ebook published in 2012 by SRA Books.

2nd Edition authored by Juanita Vorster and Roger Harrop, published in 2021.
Paperback ISBN 978-0-620-92726-0
Ebook eISBN 978-0-620-92727-7

App developer: Ralph Harris

Editing: Lizann Keuler
Cover design: Juanita Vorster
Typesetting: Liezl Strydom

Print on demand
Printing and binding by:
Groep 7 Drukkers en Uitgewers (Pty) Ltd
Pretoria, www.groep7.co.za

Roger's thanks to:
Christine LeHeup

Juanita's thanks to:
My family for unconditional support.
Roger (for allowing me to meddle).

CONTENTS

SECOND EDITION NOTES

ONE OF THE biggest challenges for anyone running – or involved in running – a business of any size in any industry is keeping an eye on all the moving parts of the business without getting stuck on any one.

Business leaders inevitably find themselves spending the greater part of their time dealing with the day-to-day and only occasionally take time to view the bigger picture. The first edition of this book was written as a guide for business leaders to make their time 'in the helicopter' as effective as possible.

This second edition adds depth and breadth to the first edition's trusted approach by including new focus areas, updated information, and practical examples based on the authors' experience (both pre- and post-pandemic).

Staying in the Helicopter® remains the ideal quick reference guide for anyone who wants to increase their business success and decrease their personal stress.

THE STORY BEHIND

THE

CEO EXPERTS™

DURING ONE OF Roger's masterclasses a delegate came up to him during a break and said: 'Roger, you really are the CEO expert, aren't you?'

The moniker stuck, and Roger started using it as part of his branding.

Fast forward to 2019 when we – Juanita, based in South Africa, and Roger, based in the UK – happened to meet at a conference in South Africa.

As we chatted, we discovered that we both had the same reason for being professional speakers: we want to make success easier for business leaders and we want to keep it simple.

So it made sense that we combine our strengths. Since then Juanita – as 'The Next CEO Expert' – adds an updated flair to Roger's wisdom that has already helped over 30 000 business leaders in over 50 countries.

For more information or to book Roger or Juanita for a keynote, seminar, masterclass, strategic planning event or to discuss consultancy advice visit **www.theceoexperts.com.**

ABOUT ROGER – THE ORIGINAL CEO EXPERT

Roger Harrop BSc(Hons), CEng, FIMechE, FCIM, FInstIB, FPSA, PSAE, CSPGlobal

Roger Harrop has spent over 25 years leading international businesses, including a Public Limited Company (PLC), which puts him in a unique position to deal with present-day business challenges.

Based in Oxford in the UK, he's an international business growth speaker who inspires and entertains audiences with his acclaimed *Staying in the Helicopter®* programmes. Over 30 000 CEOs, business leaders and others, across 50 countries, have achieved transformational change through his thought-provoking and entertaining talks laced with real-life stories and humour.

Roger is also an author, business advisor, mentor, consultant and independent director.

He has unusually wide leadership experience: from small start-ups to multi-nationals and from high-tech products to basic commodities, people-based service businesses and not-for-profit organisations.

Roger spent seven years as Group Chief Executive of a FTSE quoted, high-tech industrial group with 12 sites across four continents. The UK Government mentioned it in its 'Competitiveness' White Paper. Forbes Magazine in the US included the group among its list of the top 100 overseas companies. Two business schools have used it as a benchmark case study on culture change and business re-engineering.

Roger tutored on a leading leadership and teambuilding programme for over 25 years.

He's a keen mountain biker and classic car enthusiast.

www.rogerharrop.com

ABOUT JUANITA – THE NEXT CEO EXPERT

Juanita Vorster Cert.Dir, EO

Juanita Vorster is a successful entrepreneur with a knack for turning complex business concepts into simplified, practical advice. She also holds the designations of Certified Director and Ethics Officer.

As an 'old millennial' she has experienced the world of work how it used to be as well as where it has shifted to.

Juanita founded her own fully remote working and highly regarded outsourced marketing business in 2013. The company has reported profitable growth every year since its inception with very low churn in staff and clients. She is still very much involved in running her company and uses the lessons she learns from it to keep her advice and stories practical and fresh.

Based in South Africa, Juanita is also an international speaker, author of a number of articles in highly respected publications, a regular guest on business podcasts and a former radio programme host.

www.juanitavorster.com

A LETTER FROM US TO YOU

DEAR BUSINESS LEADER,

If you are reading this book, then it is likely that you are running a business or are in some way involved in running a business. Our experience of people like you is that you have little free time, you don't like waffle, and you like to see ideas and initiatives translated into specific, quantifiable benefits to you and your business.

That's why we kept this book short and to the point. This book includes our personal experiences with key pieces of research and models to bring you simple, profound and valuable practical tools that you can use immediately.

BEFORE YOU READ ANY FURTHER

It may not look like it, but you're holding in your hand a high-tech book with access to videos, white papers, animations, interactive business health checks and more!

We've added everything to help you stay in the 'helicopter'!

First, make sure your smartphone can read the QR codes included throughout the book. For newer model smartphones, it's as easy as opening the camera app and pointing at the QR code.

If your smartphone doesn't have a QR code reader embedded, you can download a free QR code reader from your phone's app store:

- QuickScan
- RedLaser
- ScanLife

Now, scan the QR code below to access and use this book's app.

The app contains business health checks that will help you to immediately apply what you learn in your own business.

Use the app regularly so you can view the progress of your business over time. That way you can make sure you really are flying high enough!

Scan the QR code below to access and use this book's app.

THE REAL OBJECTIVE

If you don't know where you're going, how are you ever going to get there?

MOST BUSINESS LEADERS will have spent time thinking about and developing the company vision, mission statements, strategic objectives, and plans, but they are all at a lower altitude in the 'helicopter' than where we need to start.

There is only one place to start when looking from our 'helicopter' – the business purpose.

The purpose of the business is up there at 30 000 feet and answers the question: 'What is the business there for – why does it exist?'

If you can get your purpose down to one sentence, life gets so much easier. Suddenly every strategic decision that has to be taken in the business is filtered through your business purpose. If it's not a step towards the business purpose, it simply shouldn't be done!

The purpose of a business can only be defined by the owners – the shareholders, partners or trustees.

If you're hired by the owners to run a business, you can't assume what their purpose for the business is. For listed companies, you might think that the purpose is shareholder value, but that isn't always the case, especially these days where focus has shifted to a stakeholder-inclusive approach.

If you are running a business for somebody else, you have to know what THEIR purpose for the business is.

Privately owned and family businesses can be even more complex. The original reason for setting up the business may have been lost or may have changed over time, and a new generation (with their own ideas) may have taken over.

Listen to Roger's story of how he once almost lost his job due to assuming what the purpose of a business was

I was running a masterclass for a group of 15 CEOs from various business sectors and sizes. Some were owner CEOs and some employed CEOs.

We got to the end of the morning and the chair said to one of the CEOs: 'Norman, we seemed to lose you earlier. Why?' Norman responded: 'Yes, you're right. What Roger was saying struck a chord with me. As you know, I've been running our third-generation toy business for three years – and I'm sick of it. We're getting nowhere. My father interferes, my aunt and other family members tell people what to do, and we have no idea where we're going.'

'We have a family board meeting tomorrow and I've decided to tear up the agenda and replace it with one item: purpose. And it's going to be like electing the Pope – we're going to sit there until the smoke comes out of the chimney!'

Norman rang me later that week and told me how it had gone: 'It was absolute hell – but we got there. We have all agreed on our purpose and our commitment to getting there. And do you know what? I felt the stress instantly fall from my shoulders.'

Roger

Our initial question to business owners is often: 'Is your intention to ultimately sell the business or pass it on to your successors?' They frequently answer: 'Well, if we get a good offer then we'd certainly sell.'

It simply doesn't work that way.

A fundamentally different strategy and approach is needed to successfully run a business to increase shareholder value rather than to preserve jobs, or generate cash, or maximise sustained profits or the sale value of the business.

If you wish to sell your business, let's say, for the highest possible price, then you must spend three to five years running the business in a totally different way to how you ran it before – because the purpose of the business has now changed.

When the purpose of the business is to sell it, you have to look at every area of business through a different lens.

Download the King IV Report™ on Corporate Governance to learn more about a stakeholder-inclusive approach

Grooming a Business for Sale

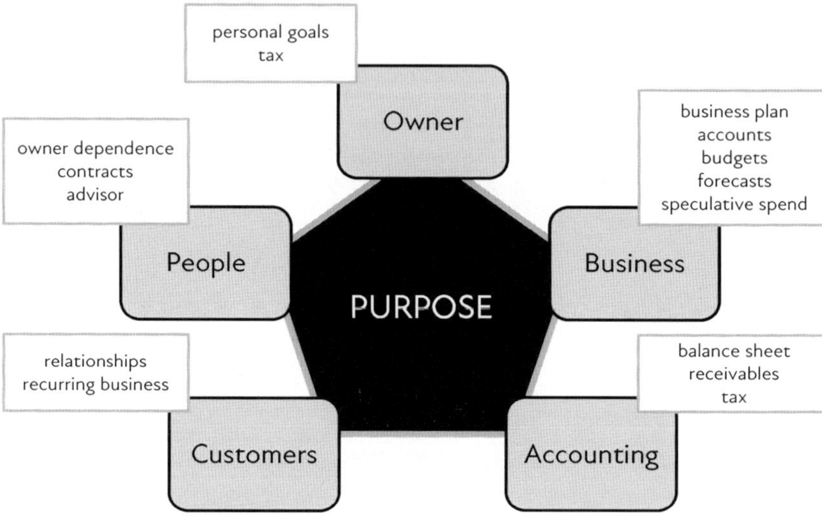

For example, you may be very proud of the fact that you've developed a culture of not giving discounts, but a potential buyer will likely pay more for your business if you have long-term contracts with your customers. That might mean that you have to negotiate on price with customers to secure those contracts.

Grooming a business for sale is incredibly difficult to do for owners who have become used to running the business because now they have to get into the mind of the potential buyer. They can't make decisions based on how they've always done it – they have a new purpose.

When a company goes through a management buyout, often a relatively ordinary group of managers seem to perform really well. Why is that? Simply because, from the moment they invest, those private equity houses or venture capitalists have just one focus: an exit in a specific number of years and a minimum percentage compound growth. And they get the entire board to have that laser beam focus.

If you can have that same laser beam focus on the purpose of your business, believe us, you stand a very good chance of getting there.

I was a non-executive director of a family business in Essex. It had been started by the father – who had passed away – and there were two sons running the business and three children not involved in the business.

When I joined, the problems were just starting off. The two sons in the business were mumbling about the additional wealth they were creating and sharing, saying that it was unfair. The ones not in the business were complaining that they never received a dividend, so they didn't see the problem.

So we set up a shareholder meeting. Remarkably, it took four shareholder meetings (with only one item on the agenda) to get to their purpose, which was sustained profitable growth with a target of 15% return on sales and 'normally pay a dividend'.

It sounds mundane, but if you look at the financial results of that business, you can see where that decision was taken – because suddenly everyone started pulling in the same direction.

Roger

If you don't know where it is you're trying to get to, how are you going to stand any chance of getting there?

When business owners start out they're crystal clear on what the business is there for, but often, over time, that purpose disappears or changes. This is because business owners never talk about purpose, or they don't do it often enough. Any shift in purpose starts causing conflict or ineffectiveness.

Often, we find that the real purpose of the business has never been discussed. It then takes an outside independent advisor or director (who can be wholly unbiased, unsentimental and objective) to ask questions of the owners and directors to tease out and reach agreement on precisely what the real purpose of the business is.

We strongly recommend that you hold a shareholder meeting for the owners of the business – not a board meeting or a management meeting – twice a year. The first item on the agenda needs to be 'Purpose' – What is our purpose TODAY?

And it's not just one purpose you need, but three:

- Financial: What are the financial goals of the business?
- Social: What difference will the business make in society? What are the values of the business?
- Brand: What role will the business play in the lives of its customers? What is the customer experience across all touchpoints?

The Three Purposes

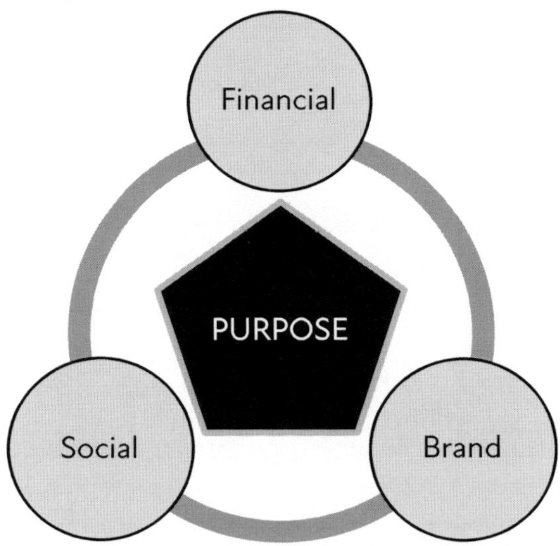

Source: 'On Purpose' by Shaun Smith and Andy Milligan

Which purpose is pre-eminent depends on the type of business.

For a commercial business the financial purpose is pre-eminent. It has to steer the business towards, for example, sustained profitable growth or cash generation or a business sale.

When we ask what the purpose is, we sometimes have business owners saying: 'Oh, mine's a lifestyle business, we're not looking to grow.'

Well, that worries us because businesses can never stand still. They either grow or contract – and they only grow if you make them grow.

I worked with a firm of architects in London with an unusual share structure. There were six shareholders – four on the board and two not. I was running a strategic retreat with their top team of about 14 people.

When I asked them what the purpose of the firm was, I got all sorts of answers. 'Save the planet', 'be the best architects in the world', and so on, until I'd filled two pages with answers.

Then, in a very quiet voice, the woman who did their internal admin said: 'I'm a shareholder in this business, and I'd quite like a return that's better than putting my money in the bank.'

The CEO exploded! 'Wow! We never thought of that before!'

He rang me up some time later and said that it had been a turning point for the business.

Too right it was!

Roger

The social purpose and values of organisations are, however, increasingly in the spotlight. People increasingly don't want to work for or buy from organisations whose values they don't share.

Companies' true values and social purpose were laid bare by the COVID-19 pandemic – there were definite heroes and villains that won't be forgotten. There is now a continued public focus on the difference between what an organisation says its purpose, focus and values are and what the organisation actually does.

For a not-for-profit organisation or a charity it is usually very clear what difference it wants to make in society. Therefore, its social purpose is pre-eminent. It's not unusual, however, that this type of organisation has insufficient focus on the financial goals that will allow it to maximise its social purpose. The term non-profit is a bit of a misnomer – it doesn't mean the organisation isn't allowed to make a profit. It simply means that the profit it makes can't be distributed to shareholders – it all has to be reinvested into the impact the organisation aims to make.

Non-profit organisations need to have clear financial goals if they are to fulfil their core purpose.

Read an excellent article on trends that are reshaping business purpose

A non-profit organisation, which was very clear on what they wanted to achieve in the community they serve, asked me to come in and help them move closer to fulfilling that purpose.

During our first session together, I asked them how much money they thought was needed to achieve everything they wanted to do. They had no idea!

The CEO eventually responded with the amount they had spent to cover their costs in the previous year. When I explained the importance of profit for non-profits organisations, the entire management team had a light-bulb moment.

At the end of the session their financial goal was five times higher, and the strategy for getting to that goal had shifted from waiting for local government funds to a much more proactive plan to get international funders involved.

Juanita

Across both the for-profit and non-profit spaces many successful organisations have been built on solving problems for customers who are willing to pay for the peace of mind that comes from having an issue taken care of.

These companies go beyond offering products and services for sale; they are crystal clear on their brand purpose – the role they want to play in the lives of their customers.

It's their customer experience that sets them apart from their competition and adds significant value to their business. We explore the topic of customer experience in our book *WIN! How to Succeed in the New Game of Business*.

The COVID-19 pandemic exponentially increased the emphasis on how important it is that organisations are driven by purpose. According to an article in The Future CEO, 79% of CEOs say that clarity on the purpose of the business has helped them understand what they need to do to meet the needs of stakeholders, employees, communities, customers, partners and investors. The article also states that purpose-led CEOs are 25% more confident in their ability to create impact through a more positive culture and higher levels of engagement.

Order your copy of WIN! How to Succeed in the New Game of Business

So, the owners of the business have to define the pre-eminent purpose of the business; they must get it down to one sentence. In everything you do, focus on this purpose like a laser beam – then you will have a very good chance of getting there.

Read the full 'CEOs with Purpose' article

Keep in mind, though, that the owners might not want to share the purpose with all stakeholders. For example, the sale of a business is typically announced only quite some time after it has become the purpose of the business.

Where we go next in our 'helicopter' is the part that is shared with ALL stakeholders.

THE FOUNDATION

Live your values every day, so you don't lose sight of them.

PEOPLE WANT TO work for, invest in, and buy from companies with which they share values.

The values of a business guide 'the way we do things around here', especially in areas where the rulebook is unclear.

These values should, of course, serve the purpose of the business as decided by the owners, and although the purpose can't always be shared with all stakeholders, the values and vision of a business should absolutely be shared.

Values shouldn't be decided in a board meeting, stuck on a website or office wall, and promptly be forgotten – they should be evident in everything the organisation does.

The habit we see most often is that business leaders pick words from a list of values that everybody else also seems to use. While respect, integrity, honesty, quality, collaboration, and so on, are noble concepts, the meaning of these concepts often differs from person to person.

A better approach is to avoid jargon and abstract concepts and rather describe 'the way we do things around here' in plain language that can guide ANY decision and action taken by ANYONE in the organisation.

Moving the values of a business from 'talk to walk' requires dedication from everyone in the business: from the chairperson to the cleaners – there can be no exceptions.

Making the values of a business easily understandable and consistently visible will make it easier for employees, customers, investors, and so on, to decide if they want to make your business part of their lives.

Increasingly, the majority of these stakeholders want a company's values to align to ethical standards that aim to protect and preserve individuals, communities and natural resources.

Fashion house Burberry lived their value of 'commitments to communities' by turning their trench coat factory in Castleford in the UK to manufacturing personal protection equipment (PPE) for medical and care workers. The company donated more than 100 000 pieces of PPE to the National Health Service early in the COVID-19 pandemic.

Even before the pandemic, companies started seeing how important defining, sharing and living values are. BP CEO Bernard Looney admitted: 'There's no question that we would not have been able to hire the people we have in the last six months had we not laid out our ambition to become a net-zero carbon company.'

Two of the UK's biggest investors decided not buy shares in the delivery company Deliveroo because of concerns over Deliveroo riders' rights. The company maintains that the legal status of their riders is self-employed contractors rather than employees, but investors hold firm that they will not support such an unsustainable way of approaching workers' rights.

In addition to consistently living the values of the business, you also have to deal swiftly with anything in the business that doesn't align with those values – that includes any activity from employees, suppliers and other strategic partners.

Remember, in the eyes of the world what you allow is what you condone.

'It felt like everything was breaking at once.' That's how Brian Chesky, co-founder and CEO of Airbnb, explains what happened when they lost sight of the company's values. The COVID-19 pandemic triggered a billion-dollar loss for the company. This forced Airbnb to get back to its roots and find a balance between what works for customers, for people who depend on Airbnb for income, and for the cities they operate in.

Defining the values of the business and sharing them for everyone to see and experience builds a strong foundation for where we go next in our 'helicopter'.

THE DIRECTION

Share the vision regularly, so all can see the golden uplands you are targeting.

BUSINESSES THAT SHOW sustained profitable growth don't express their aspirations based on the way things have always been – and they don't accept industry norms. The vision and aspiration of business leaders should, of course, align with the purpose and values of the business, but they don't have to align with market average.

One of the biggest decisions business leaders have to make is what price they charge – and it shouldn't be what everyone else is charging!

> In 1987, Red Bull was started by Dietrich Mateschitz, an Austrian who had seen tuk-tuk drivers in Bangkok drinking various home-brewed concoctions to keep them going through the day. Unable to raise bank finance for his 'energy drink' (an entirely new concept at the time), he borrowed a few thousand euros from his family and got the company off the ground.
>
> Red Bull is now sold in more than 150 countries around the world as a high-caffeine, carbonated soft drink. Even though the caffeine content of one regular can of Red Bull is pretty much the same as one cup of coffee, it sells at almost six times the price of regular soda!
>
> Red Bull didn't achieve this remarkable success by focusing on the average. They must have roughly the same production costs as regular

soda manufacturers and yet the margins they're making are phenomenal.

These days, there are so many examples of organisations that went from nothing to, incredibly quickly, dominating the world. It all comes down to how big business leaders can dream.

Never run the business according to preconceived ideas.

In every company I've ever run, my finance director or CFO would come to me, at some point, and say: 'Look at the margins we're making! They're 2.5% better than industry average or 2% better than our biggest competitor.'

I'd always tell them that I'm not interested in those numbers because we're not going to set our standards by industry average and what our competitors are doing!

Roger

Leaders who are self-limiting in their aspiration for the business are often more of a threat to sustained profitable growth than economic pressures and fluctuating trends.

Business leaders need to be driven by great aspiration. They need to create a culture of 'failing forward' so that everything in the business consistently aligns to the aspiration. You need to be so inspired by your own aspirational belief, passion and courage that others can't resist joining the journey.

You and your business can do anything! It's up to you.

Of course, having great aspiration and a positive mindset is only the start – now, you have to put it into practice. The next level for our 'helicopter' is where we look at the different ways a business can become a world leader.

THE SHAPE

A business must never be all things to all people.

HAVING CLEARLY ESTABLISHED the purpose, values and aspiration of the business, we now have to look at its principal drivers.

Statistically, market leaders are more successful than anybody else, so it's worthwhile looking at what makes them tick. For their book *The Discipline of Market Leaders* Michael Treacy and Fred Wiersema extensively researched market-leading companies across a wide range of market sectors worldwide – from SMEs to multinational corporations.

Their conclusions are fundamentally simple: to be a market leader you need to be a leader in one of three basic drivers and at least industry average in the other two:

- operational excellence
- product or process innovation
- customer intimacy

Access more information on The Discipline of Market Leaders book

OPERATIONAL EXCELLENCE

The essence of this driver is being the lowest-cost provider in the market. The types of company driven by operational excellence are commodity businesses, budget airlines, fast food restaurants, and so on. They are characterised by:

- optimised supply chain processes
- standardised, simplified, tightly controlled operations and decision systems
- customers receiving reliable high-speed transactions
- a 'lean and mean' culture where operational efficiency is highly rewarded
- approaches to continuous improvement are deeply ingrained
- selling on price

A 'command and control' leadership style often works best in these types of organisation, as the focus is on getting it all to run with military discipline. These companies want people who can work hard and complete tasks exactly as they were trained to do – free thinkers often do not feel welcome here.

For these companies, it's imperative to know in intimate detail not only the cost but also the profitability of every transaction in the business.

Watch how a budget airline in South Africa proved the industry wrong by focusing on operational excellence

I worked with a company that sells timber and wooden products. Talking with the CEO, I asked what sort of metrics they had in place to measure business success. The CEO said, for example, their largest customer demanded that they deliver within a two-hour window, 24 hours a day, seven days a week, 364 days a year.

I asked how they had performed the year before, and the CEO said it had been an absolute disaster. They'd only achieved 87.57% on time, and, as a result, no one got a pay raise or a bonus. But the CEO was confident that they would make the current year's target, which was 90.07%.

After spending five days in the company, I realised that absolutely everyone in the business spoke to two decimal places – they were that focused on operational excellence.

Roger

If you're selling your standard product on price, then you've got to spend every waking moment getting your costs down and improving profitability because your price is absolutely fixed.

Often, of course, customers who want a non-standard product or service will pay a significant premium to get what they want from a business driven by operational excellence.

PRODUCT OR PROCESS INNOVATION

Companies driven by product innovation push the boundaries of the market with innovative products and processes. Apple, Dyson, 3M and big pharmaceutical companies are great examples of this. For Amazon, it was the process of buying books that was initially innovative.

These types of business generate anticipation and excitement among customers – often long before a launch. Their products or services are never sold as the cheapest on the market but rather at a premium based on perceived added value. They are characterised by:

- a focus on invention, product development, and market exploitation
- adaptable structures that encourage internal entrepreneurism
- reward for new product successes
- tolerance of failure
- seeking to create new markets by going beyond currently articulated needs

Watch how 3M embodies the characteristics of product leadership

The leaders of these companies tolerate – and often celebrate – failures in the pursuit of the next big thing. The ongoing search for the next big thing is the biggest challenge for a company driven by product leadership – new ideas have to come along as if they're on a treadmill, and they've got to be at least as good as the ones they replace.

The success of these companies isn't judged by their past wins, but on their pipeline of new products and innovation.

The leadership style and key performance indicators (KPIs) of this type of business are far different from those for a business driven by operational excellence.

CUSTOMER INTIMACY

A business driven by customer intimacy does everything it can to develop the relationship with its chosen and most valuable customers. They focus on:

- identifying customer problems
- developing and identifying solutions to customer problems
- empowering customer-facing employees
- carefully selecting and nurturing clients
- a solution-based culture that thrives on dedicated repeat customers
- organisational versatility to customise products and services

Take a look at what the customers of Rackspace Technology have to say about the company's 'fanatical support'

These companies don't just accept anyone as customer – they choose their customers and give those customers what they value most.

Professional services and consulting firms are usually driven by customer intimacy. Some supermarkets have also adopted a customer intimacy model and people happily pay more for the same products just because of the experience they have going into that type of store.

Until you've made a clear decision on the target shape of the business and you have everyone signed up to that target shape, it is not unusual for assumptions to be made as to the drivers of the business. To start, you need to check the current shape of the business.

Make a cross in the boxes that are most true for your business. Remember, you cannot be a leader in more than one discipline.

The Shape of the Business

What shape *are we now*?

	Operational Excellence	Product or Process Innovation	Customer Intimacy
Market Leader			
Fast Follower			
Industry Average			
Below Average			

What shape *do we want to be*?

	Operational Excellence	Product or Process Innovation	Customer Intimacy
Market Leader			
Fast Follower			
Industry Average			
Below Average			

You can also complete the Shape of the Business grids in our app

Now that you know the shape you want the business to be, it's time to look at what must change for you to become a market leader in the discipline you chose – operational excellence, product or process innovation, or customer intimacy.

Once you've gone through this process, every significant decision you make you should be filtered through the question: 'Is this a step towards the desired shape of the business or not?'

Life will get much easier as a result!

I worked with a fairly sizable cold rolled steel manufacturing company near Birmingham. They'd been able to move away from being a commodities business driven by operational excellence to being driven by product and process innovation.

I had the board of directors, top management and the salesforce in the room, and everybody agreed that they were driven by product and process innovation.

To test this, I asked: 'So you never sell on price?' Somebody answered: 'We do sell on price for the legacy products we've had for years as well as to our loyal customers.'

We then had a long discussion where we said that a salesforce can't sell on both price and product innovation – they will always sell everything on price simply because it's easier. At the end, we agreed that they had two options.

The first option was to drop the legacy products completely and take the hit. I told them that, although I couldn't prove it, I believed very strongly that if they got rid of the legacy products, they would be much more successful with the other products because they could focus on selling only on product innovation.

The second option was to split the legacy products into a second division driven by operational excellence.

From that point on, they looked at their business completely differently because they could now make a decision based on the ideal shape of the business.

Roger

Always remember, only if you are driven by operational excellence do you sell on price. Organisations driven by product leadership or customer excellence are selling perceived added value and they sell it at a premium.

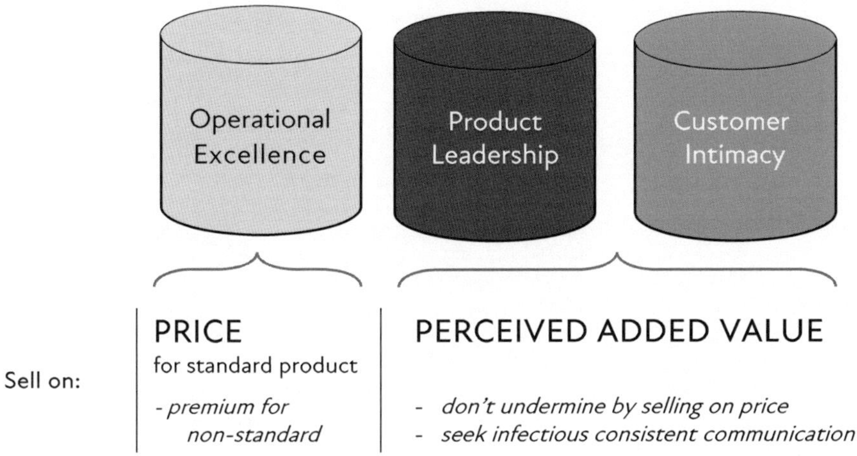

Whichever discipline you choose to be a market leader in, always do it according to your greatest aspirations, not according to what your competitors are doing. Your offer needs to be innovative and, if possible, change the rules of your whole industry or profession.

To do this, we suggest that you regularly meet with the six to eight most lateral thinkers in your organisation – never mind what jobs they have – and put them in a room for a couple of hours with no interruptions and plenty of flipcharts. If these people are spread across the world, then get them into an online meeting and let them collaborate on a shared online tool like Google Workspace.

Let nothing stand in your (or their) way to challenge the paradigms of the business, products, processes, markets, sectors, routes to market, and every aspect of what you do and why you do it. We guarantee that sooner or later those sessions will yield a golden nugget of an idea that sets you on the route to being a market leader.

I was invited to run a strategic retreat for the trustees and top team of a major charity. Based on the briefing I had received from the CEO, I decided to discuss their business drivers early on. I split them into three teams and asked each group to discuss and agree on the current shape of the charity and their target for the future.

Each group reported back, and, remarkably, one group was clear that they should be driven by product/process leadership, another said operational excellence, and the third, customer intimacy!

I tore up my plans for the rest of the event. We spent our time discussing only this, and by the end we had an agreed target shape.

Some months later the CEO called me to say that this had been a major turning point for them and that they had gone from strength to strength thereafter. 'I hadn't realised' she said, 'that we were all pulling in different directions, whereas now we are not and that has empowered us to really achieve.'

Roger

Keep checking the shape of the business by asking yourself:

- What does the heartbeat of the business say about where the focus and energy is?
- Have you made a clear choice about the shape of the business?
- Are you targeting customer groups who value this shape?
- Is everyone in the organisation aligned with the chosen shape?
- Are you always looking to move the benchmarks upwards?

The chosen shape of the business is the departure point for where we go next in our 'helicopter': answering the big question of 'Why should we buy from you?'

THE DIFFERENTIATORS

Customers want to buy solutions, not specifications.

WHAT IS YOUR value proposition – what differentiates you? What are the three reasons why customers should buy from you rather than your competitors?

If you're driven by operational excellence, the number one reason might be price, but for customer intimacy and product or process innovation driven businesses **none** of the three reasons is price.

While speaking at a conference for leasing agents, I talked about value proposition. I shared with them that I was a landlord with a number of properties and what I wanted to hear in order to choose an agent for these properties. I said that I'd like to hear: 'We want to maximise your income', 'We will anticipate problems so that you don't have void periods' and 'We have a database of the most reliable tenants'.

I said that over years of using many agents, I had never heard or read any of these things. Furthermore, I told them that I'd looked at many of their websites and I hadn't seen anything like that. I had 150 people staring at me with their mouths open!

Roger

The value proposition isn't a list of things the business can do: it's a summary of the impact its products and services has on the lives of its customers – whether in business-to-consumer (B2C) or business-to-business (B2B) settings. This requires an in-depth knowledge of who the ideal customer for the business is and what their needs are.

I worked with a professional services company that had undertaken a strategic review of their services and brand positioning. During the process, they asked for my opinion on their main company brochure.

It was a typical multiple page document filled to the brim with everything all their competitors also had in their brochures – history, vision and mission statements, achievements, services, and so on. Nothing in that document answered the question 'Why should I buy from you?'

So we spent some time on transforming their 'specification' statements about what they do into 'solution' statements about how their services solve the biggest problems their clients usually face. The result was a simplified company brochure that very clearly set them apart from their competitors.

Juanita

Have a look at the elements of value for ***B2C*** *customers (might require sign-in)*

As with the values of the business, the value proposition should be stated in plain language. At the drop of a hat, everyone in the organisation should be able to share the three reasons for 'Why people should buy from us.' They should also know what their role is in living up to the promises the value proposition makes.

The value proposition should be the strongest arrow in the quiver of your salespeople – they must be able to use it to close deals without giving any discount.

The prices quoted by your salespeople prices should reflect the shape and value proposition of the business, and this is where we focus next.

*Have a look at the elements of value for **B2B** customers (might require sign-in)*

THE PRICES

If you're good at what you do, then you deserve higher prices, not discounts!

WE'VE DISCUSSED THE drivers of business, and, whichever it is for you, it should change the way you think about prices. If you're driven by operational excellence, you sell on price, but only for the standard product. You have to ensure that a customer who requires something non-standard always pays a significant premium.

If you're driven by product leadership or customer intimacy you do not sell on price but at a premium based upon your perceived added value. You have to assume that every single buyer you're selling to is trying to turn your offering into a commodity – it's their job to buy at the lowest price. The job of your salespeople is to do exactly the opposite: to turn the perception of whatever it is they're selling into an added value product or service.

When we work with organisations on a consultation basis, one of the first things we do is to ask the CEO for a full-year margin report presented as two tables: one listing customers and one listing product lines. We then ask that each table be sorted so that the lowest percentage margin is at the top and the highest percentage margin at the bottom.

Almost always, the CEO is shocked by just how low margin some customers and some product lines have been.

We then discuss and agree with the CEO on the minimum percentage margin they would like to set. Every customer below that minimum percentage is assigned an A, B or C rating. These ratings are allocated based on consideration of each individual customer or product line: the history, maintenance effort, realised value, and so on.

- For A-rated customers or product lines, prices are to be increased immediately to achieve the agreed minimum percentage – no matter the consequences.
- For B-rated customers or product lines, the same is applied more gently over a 12-month period.
- For C-rated customers or product lines, a fixed end date is set. If the additional business has not been achieved by the set date, that customer or product line reverts to an A rating.

Each time we've gone through this process with clients the result has been a significant increase in margins and rarely any loss of goodwill from customers.

Most of us undervalue what we do. Ask yourself: 'Are we good at what we do?'. If you are, then you deserve higher prices, and that belief should be reflected in the DNA of your company.

Set your prices and don't allow salespeople to give discounts! Your prices are where they are because of the value you give.

Instead of agreeing to discount, rather offer 'stuff' that is of high perceived value to the customer but that costs you nothing or very little. Sales management should be clear on the list of things salespeople can offer other than discounts.

I worked with a number of recruitment companies that were in the habit of giving 20% discounts.

I took them through an exercise of thinking about 'stuff' they could add to their offering to increase the perceived added value. One guy mentioned that they have a license to do unlimited psychometric tests, so instead of agreeing to discounts, they should offer free psychometric testing for each candidate.

Every business has 'stuff' to give, you just need to put a bit of time into it.

Roger

Many of us have price books, which, historically, note the different discounts given to customers, or for specific order values, or whatever. Please, do take the time to inspect these and ask why and whether, today, there is justification for these discounts.

In our *Staying in the Helicopter®* masterclass we ask business leaders: 'What would happen if you put up your prices by just 1% tomorrow morning?'

The response we get from the majority is usually: 'Probably nothing'.

So, the question has to be: 'Why don't you do it?'. That 1% will go straight on the bottom line for you to reinvest in the growth of the business.

I ran a masterclass for the top team and branch managers of one of the largest builders' merchants in the UK.

This is not a sector of high margins and is one that I would have thought was price sensitive. Nevertheless, I asked a number of the branch managers individually what the consequences would be if they increased their net prices by 1% the next day. The response from each was that they did not think there would be any effect. I then asked why they hadn't already done it. They answered that it was probably just the fear that they might lose some customers.

I looked at the CEO and sat down: 20 minutes later they had all agreed to put their prices up by 2% the next day.

I checked with them some weeks later, and, as far as they could tell, they had lost no customers.

Roger

Remember, it's our job as business leaders to take risks to achieve our strategic objectives. If you don't focus on every opportunity to increase prices and improve margins, you cannot assume anyone else in your team will.

What we have a look at next from our 'helicopter' is some more left-brain stuff – measuring progress in line with the chosen shape of the business.

THE MEASUREMENTS

Don't let your accountants run the business.

ACCOUNTANTS – JUST like most professions – can make their activities appear more complex and difficult to understand than necessary. Whilst they do need to make complex calculations and provide complex reports to stick to laws and regulations, they must also be able to give you the right financial and non-financial KPIs when you want and in the way you want, so you can run the business efficiently.

Regardless of what others may say, financial information is there simply to help you run the business.

TERMINOLOGY

It is your responsibility to ensure that you get the numbers for the business in the format, level of detail and terminology you want.

Each of these terms can mean exactly the same:

- orders = bookings
- order book = backlog
- backlog = overdue orders = back orders (sometimes)
- sales = revenue = turnover = income
- cost of goods sold = cost of sales

- gross profit = trading profit = contribution
- earnings before interest, taxes, depreciation and amortisation (EBITDA) = profit before interest and tax (PBIT) (sometimes) = operating profit = trading profit = earnings before interest and taxes (EBIT) = surplus
- earnings (sometimes) = earnings before tax (EBT) = profits before tax (PBT) = net profit
- receivables = debtors
- payables = creditors
- inventory = stock (sometimes)
- cash = liquidity
- work in progress = work in process
- profit and loss account (P&L) = income statement

We sent this list to a dozen financial people around the world. They all came back with some very pedantic statements to explain that certain terms were definitely not equivalent and had quite different meanings. The problem was, these pedantic statements didn't agree with each other on what each term meant!

You need to get into your helicopter and take control! Decide which accounting terms you want to adopt, then make everyone – including your accountants and auditors – stick with them in everything you and they do.

For the purposes of this book we will be using the first term of each set in the above terminology list.

Having got your terminology fixed, the next thing you need to be clear on is the information you need, and how and when you want it presented.

MONTHLY REPORTS

Your monthly reporting pack – yes, even the smallest business should have one – is only there to help you and your team run the business and measure how you're doing. There is no legal requirement that defines what it should look like, so you have to decide what information and format make sense for your unique business.

It is so easy to get bogged down in the detailed numbers and miss the big picture – we've seen this more in large corporates than smaller organisations. Being presented with the accounts exactly as your accountants traditionally prepare them may not be right for you.

For example, accountants traditionally present a profit and loss account with sales at the top and profit at the bottom. That's the exact reverse of the importance most of us should be putting on the numbers!

The figures you see in a set of accounts are, by definition, historical. But what you need to do to run the business effectively is look to the future.

I worked for Burmah Oil at one time, and their monthly reporting packs and annual budget papers were up to 50 pages long! They were not drawn up in any way to help the CEO run the business.

When I was at BTR, the reverse was true. They had the most outstanding monthly reporting pack I had come across – it was never more than ten pages, and the first page summary gave an instant overview of the business from which you could then drill down into areas of concern as necessary.

I've since used a development of that format in many companies and for clients.

If you'd like a copy, just drop me an email: **roger@rogerharrop.com**

Roger

Running a business successfully is as much about looking at trends as at the absolute figures.

The monthly report should start with a summary sheet of both financial and non-financial information shown month on month – ideally tracked against last year and your budget. This should give you sufficient trend indications to instantly see the health of the business and how things are going.

Financial Measures

So, what financial information do you need on this all-important monthly summary sheet?

- Start with what's most important: **profit** (assuming your purpose in some way embraces profitable growth).
- If you're in the type of business where there is a time lag between receiving the order and making the sale, you need **order input**, as this is the very first indication of what's going on in the business.
- Also have an **order book** so you can see what you've got to go at.
- **Return on sales** (ROS) (discussed later in this chapter).
- Depending on the business, one or two **balance sheet items**, which should always include **receivables**.
- **People numbers.**
- **Cash flow**. We saw the importance of having cash available during the COVID-19 pandemic. Many hugely profitable businesses had to drastically reduce staff or even cease operations simply because they didn't have the cash necessary to tide them over during periods of lockdown.
- **Control of working capital** – essentially receivables, payables and inventory – is very important for you to monitor. You should regularly look at accounts receivable days and inventory days (where appropriate) and do regular cash flow forecasting, which really isn't hard to do with a reasonable degree of accuracy no matter what business you are in.

Non-Financial Measures

We firmly believe in the adage 'If you don't measure it, you're unlikely to improve it.' You will, therefore, also need some non-financial measures.

Some of these measures are KPIs that follow directly from the business drivers of operational excellence, product/process leadership, and customer intimacy.

If you are driven by operational excellence, for example, you may give prominence to measures like OTIF (delivery on time in full) and transaction cost.

Companies driven by product leadership often set targets for the percentage of annual sales derived from new products and highlight that monthly.

In companies driven by customer intimacy, a customer satisfaction measure may take centre stage.

Other KPIs you may want to highlight include:

- health & safety index
- quality measure
- sustainability index
- service levels achieved
- people churn
- employee happiness (Roger has seen TINYpulse used to successfully survey this)

Visit the TINYpulse website

> In one of the companies I ran, we decided to set ourselves three testing targets (that we believed to be realistic).
>
> These were for at least 30% of sales to come from products introduced in the last three years, at least 25% of sales to come from new customers, and to increase export sales from a current 12% to over 75% in three years.

> We set up KPIs to measure these three metrics and monitored them constantly. It was no coincidence that we achieved two of the three and came very close to the third.
>
> Roger

ANNUAL BUDGETING

Experience consistently shows that businesses that have the discipline of putting together a simple three-year business plan and a budget each year are more successful than those who don't – no matter the size or type of business.

As we know for the vast majority of us profit is our number one focus (rather than sales), so the first we recommend is:

Don't call it a budget, call it a 'profit plan'.

Roger has had many, many profit plans and budgets presented to him for approval, and a good number of these have been what he calls 'salesperson's plans'. Such plans are predicated on one assumption only: sales volumes are going to increase, which will in turn generate improved profits.

These are not robust profit plans. They are likely to be missed – and missed badly – since what you often find is that overheads and people numbers have been allowed to increase on the back of predicted sales growth. When that growth doesn't happen as forecast, it's a double whammy hit on profitability.

For a profit plan to be robust and stand a good chance of being achieved, it needs to represent a three-legged stool.

The incremental increase in profit (for which you are planning in your profit plan) needs to come equally from each of the legs, or the stool will fall over.

The Basis of a Robust Profit Plan

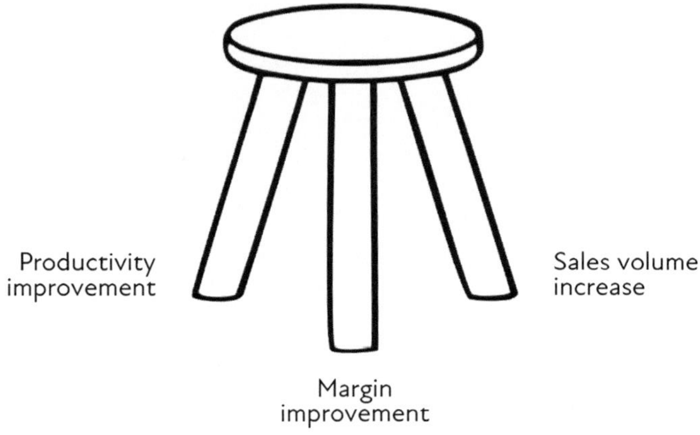

Productivity improvement is the better use of people.

In our masterclass *Electrify your Profitability*™, we have our delegates be the board of an imaginary company, and we take them through a robust profit plan process. It is not unusual, after discussion, for them to tell us they are convinced that it would be possible to get up to 30% more sales volume through the business with no change in people spend!

Margin improvement comes solely from properly evaluated price increases on the one hand and cost savings on the other.

Sales volume is just that: an increase in the top line before any price increases.

As a final check on whether the profit plan you've put together (or which is being presented to you) makes sense and is achievable, we recommend that you draw up a simple helicopter P&L account with only the following seven elements:

- orders
- sales
- materials or costs (excluding all labour)
- payroll and associated costs
- depreciation

- all other overheads
- profit (EBITDA)

This type of P&L statement is particularly valuable when you are reviewing a profit plan submitted to you for approval.

If you're in the manufacturing business, as likely as not, you will have some element of labour and factory overhead in your product costing and gross margin calculation. This can make true year on year comparisons difficult. So, for such a business, you will need to include a further line of labour, overhead, and materials going in or coming out of stock (just one figure) and then ensure all people costs are in the payroll line to complete the P&L statement.

If your purpose embraces sustained profitable growth, then a key performance indicator is ROS, which is EBITDA as a percentage of sales.

$$\textit{Return on Sales} = \frac{\textit{EBITDA}}{\textit{Sales}}\ \%$$

You need to ensure not only that your absolute profit figure increases year on year but also that your ROS improves every single year.

For that to happen, one or more of the elements below the sales level in the P&L (materials, payroll, other overheads, depreciation) must be reduced as a percentage of sales each year.

Therefore, the key ratios to look at in the helicopter P&L, when comparing, say, a profit plan for next year with forecast performance for the current year, are simply the individual line ratios against sales – because only by reducing each of those can the ROS increase. It really is that simple!

In the example below, on first sight, the proposed budget looks reasonable with the EBITDA improving by over 10%. However, when you look at the ROS it is budgeted to go down by two percentage points. You should never allow that to happen without very good reason.

	Full year			
	Actual this year (000s)		Budget next year (000s)	
Orders	5150		6600	
Sales	4500		5750	
Materials	1845	41.0%	2358	41.0%
Payroll	720	16.0%	1092	19.0%
Depreciation	180	4.0%	250	4.3%
Other overheads	1080	24.0%	1200	22.6%
EBITDA	675		750	
ROS	15.0%		13.0%	

On inspection we can see that while the margin (materials/sales %) has been maintained and the other overheads ratio has gone down (as it should with increased sales volume), there is a significant increase in payroll costs as a percentage of sales budgeted. Why? Is there a plan to pay big bonuses or take on additional people – or are they trying to squirrel away some 'contingency funds'!

There we have it: a helicopter methodology that should work for you to achieve your business purpose.

We can hear you saying to yourself that it's all very interesting, but that you can really rely on your accountant, finance director or controller to do all this analysis and monitoring for you, and that you shouldn't need to worry about it.

Please do not make that assumption – it's very dangerous.

It's your job to run your business, and that means it's your job to keep a grip on the key numbers and trends.

The target of most businesses is (often elusive) profitable growth. Assuming margins and costs are under control, it's reasonable to conclude that profitable growth is principally dependent on sales growth – the next level we hover at in our 'helicopter'.

THE CUSTOMERS

*Make it easy for customers to buy from you…
and to keep buying from you.*

POST-COVID-19, MARKETS ARE changing faster than ever before. Customer well-being is also changing more rapidly: the needs of customers and potential customers are changing and therefore new companies addressing new markets are appearing at a rapid pace.

This merely reinforces that we must never allow ourselves or our people to get comfortable. We must challenge and seek out opportunities like never before and always remind ourselves of a golden rule of business:

Sell to people who have money.

If your usual customers no longer have money don't try and sell to them! Find new customers or new markets whose problems you can solve.

To solve their problems, we need to continually assess every single touchpoint with our customers and potential customers, their current needs, and our offerings. We must then address any weak points identified.

Read more about how global trends affect who has money and how your salespeople should spend their time in our book WIN! How to Succeed in the New Game of Business

From our 'helicopter', the Customer Hourglass model is a great visual checklist.

Customer Hourglass

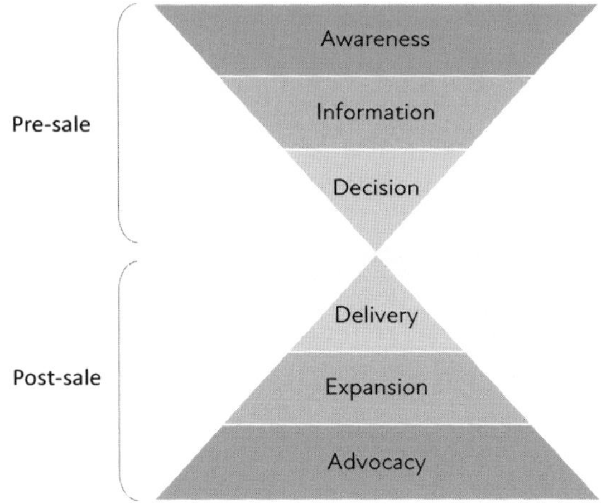

PRE-SALE

In our chapter 'The Shape', we talk about the need to choose your customers. If, for example, you put massive effort into being the market leader in customer intimacy, we simply don't want customers who buy on price. Similarly, if you are driven by product leadership, you need to focus on customers who value that product leadership.

In addition to making your chosen customers aware of your organisation, you also need to make potential customers acutely aware of your three value propositions.

When it comes to marketing and promotion to create awareness, customer-facing professions get very excited about the latest tools, tricks, buzz words, acronyms, jargon and often the most complex of marketing activities. Digital advertising, for example, makes up over 50% of total advertising spend in the US, but that doesn't necessarily mean it's right for your business.

When thinking about a promotional programme of any kind, you need to 'think outside the box'. The most successful campaigns are often the most creative and innovative – and they don't need to be expensive. You must be absolutely sure that you're using the right media and marketing mechanisms for you in a way that is attractive to your target customers and their changing needs.

Once potential customers become aware of your business and what you offer, they will look for more detailed information.

When did you last check that the information available to potential customers is correct and paints the best possible picture of your business? And is this true for both your offline and online marketing material?

I worked with a client who wanted to increase sales of their cornerstone product. I asked to see the marketing material on the product and found that it hadn't been updated in years, even though the company had recently changed its name and updated its corporate identity!

The CEO was astonished that the marketing department had only applied the new branding to new brochures – they hadn't even thought of updating old marketing brochures. Their reason? 'We're going to finish the old stock before we print new ones.'

While their cost-saving intent was noble, they didn't think about how potential customers might be put off by the outdated and old-fashioned marketing material.

Information about the business should make sense to potential customers, not only to the salespeople of the business.

Juanita

Have a look at what 'guerrilla marketing' can do for your business

Discovery/Purchase Process

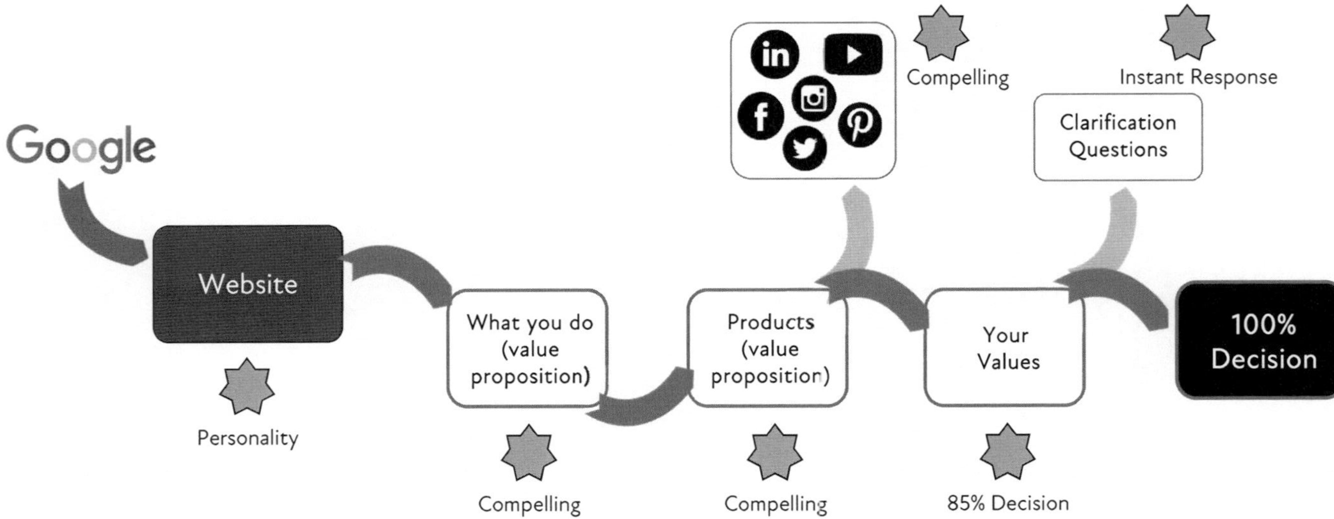

©theceoexperts.com

Research has shown that in an increasing number of market sectors 85% of buying decisions are made before any contact is made with the company!

What does this mean for you? Among other things, it means that your website and online offerings are orders of magnitude more important than they used to be, but it's much more than that. It's an evolution in our customers' process of discovering what we have to offer and how they make their purchasing decisions.

These days, when someone has a problem, whether it's B2C or B2B, one of the first places they look for a solution is Google.

So, to have any chance of being seen you need to 'own' your Google presence. That means you need to appear at or near the top of the Google search results relevant to your products & services, and you've got to set up your online presence in a way that tells Google exactly what you can do for customers.

Find out which words and phrases your target customers use when they search for what you do. Then make sure those words and phrases are used regularly and logically in the text on your website and elsewhere online.

If you run that search on Google you need to appear on the first screen – no scrolling down or going to the next results page, or that potential client will have already pursued someone else.

Don't assume that your marketing and IT people are already doing this – you need to make sure that they do.

Assuming they've found you, your potential customer's next stop is your website.

The first thing your website must do is reflect the culture and personality of the business – and, in our experience, a great many websites don't do that!

The best way to test this is to read what's on your website aloud: if it doesn't sound like your business, change it! This is not a job to just leave to your marketing people – you have to get involved.

The words and ease of use of your website need to be compelling.

Your website has to say what you do in plain language. Very few of us do that. We use industry jargon and acronyms, or we assume that anyone visiting the website already understands what we do.

You've also got to give your website visitors a reason to stay on the site. Right from the start, make a compelling case for why they should buy from you rather than anyone else. Your three value propositions (as we discuss in 'The Differentiators' chapter) need to come across strongly to any visitor to your site. Remember, at this point, you don't even know they're looking at your website, so you have no way of influencing them – other than with what is there.

Visitors will look at your individual products and services and want to know why one offer is more expensive than another, why one model will work better for a certain type of use, and so on. And, once again, it's got to be clear why they should buy from you and not from your competitors!

Visitors will then leave your website for a while to look at what other people say about you on review websites and social media. You therefore cannot afford to ignore social media – your customers are using it to make up their minds on whether they're going to buy from you or not!

A friend of mine runs a training company that works solely with top banks. He told me that they had recently received a big, three-year contract from one of them. When he met the buyer, he asked: 'Why us?' She replied that it had been very close, and they had been unable to choose between two organisations. 'In the end,' she said, 'I had a look at your personal LinkedIn profile and that of the CEO of the other company. You had more recommendations, so you got the business.'

Roger

Social media is not where you go to overtly sell what you've got to offer: it's where you go to demonstrate the value of what you have and to build trust with your potential customers.

While we're on the subject of social media, we've got to mention video. It's an increasingly powerful marketing tool that shows up at the top of Google and social media search results – and it doesn't have to be expensive. People would rather have a best-effort amateur video that helps them get to know your organisation than no video at all. You should have a YouTube channel populated with all kinds of videos about your products, your organisation, and its people and values.

Our final words on social media – because we really could go on for days – is that you need to make sure you know how the most popular social media platforms work. At the very least, have your own active LinkedIn profile. Social media has always been less about technology and more about communication – use these free platforms to your advantage!

Once your potential customers are satisfied with what they've seen about you and that your products and services do what they promise to, and they feel more familiar with your brand, they'll return to your website and look at your values.

People increasingly want to work with and buy from organisations whose values they share.

Read how one CEO let his employees and their partners create the company's values

Your values need to be authentic, real, practical and true to you. There are no values that are better or worse than others: values cannot be prescribed, and they don't have to conform to any standard other than what is already embedded in your organisation.

Have a good look at the whole organisation and find words that accurately describe what everyone pays attention to and works hard at – not just the big things but the small things too. The values that appear obvious or small to you might just be really important to someone reading about it on your website.

This brings visitors to having made about 85% of their buying decision – and you still don't even know that they're considering buying from you!

If they like what they've seen so far, they might have some clarifying questions – and here's where so many organisations drop the ball.

We regularly test the 'contact us' button on client websites before we present a *Staying in the Helicopter*® masterclass. The results have been pretty consistent – about two out of 10 get back to us within 24 hours, four out of 10 get back to us with unhelpful generic replies, and the remaining four never even acknowledge our requests.

That's simply not good enough!

You've got to set up metrics for how fast and how well queries coming from your website are answered. The same goes for the messages sent to your social media pages. Remember, everything the potential customer has done up to this 85% decision point has taken them, probably, minutes rather than hours.

You must be able to use whatever media the client would prefer to use – chat bot, WhatsApp, Facebook, LinkedIn or Instagram message, phone or email – and always with a friendly smile!

Research has shown that most people born after 1990 carry out every transaction in their life – private and business – through their smartphone. If your business website and processes are not smartphone friendly, these people quite simply won't buy from you.

By the time people contact you for more information, you must assume they are on the verge of buying from you. Not answering their questions or answering late or with generic information is as good as throwing money down the drain.

Only once you've answered all their questions will they reach a 100% buying decision. This could be to buy what they need from you, take the next step of setting up a sales meeting, or ask you to register on a vendor list.

MAKING THE SALE

From our 'helicopter', it's beneficial to remind ourselves of the basic truths of successful selling:

- The very best salespeople spend 90% of their time on the customer relationship and only 10% on trying to sell them something.
- Successful selling often depends more on the enthusiasm and belief exhibited by the salesperson than on their technical sales skills and product knowledge.
- Everyone in your business who has any kind of contact with customers must be trained as a salesperson.

Interestingly, we are seeing a renaissance in organisations having potential suppliers pitch to them in person (after they've done the work online). You can increase your pitch success dramatically by following the tried and tested rules we explain in our book *WIN! How to Succeed in the New Game of Business*.

If your offering is however sold via e-commerce, you don't have the benefit of relying on the trust and relationship built during personal interactions. The bottom half of the Customer Hourglass model is therefore even more important!

Read about the best way to pitch in our book WIN! How to Succeed in the New Game of Business

POST-SALE

Organisations often put tremendous focus on – and significant investment into – the generation of new customers above all else, but there are other ways to grow the business that involve less risk, less investment, and have more likelihood of success.

Growing the business through existing customers starts with the bare minimum of keeping the promises made during the sales period.

You can't afford to have a disconnect between what the salespeople sold and what the business delivers!

We are increasingly seeing that exceptional organisations differentiate themselves from the competition by offering products or services that consistently exceed the expectations of customers, and they offer it in a way that is almost frictionless.

You must strive to achieve outstanding levels of service to your customers if they are to remain loyal and, even better, become advocates for you. You also need a plan for how you're going to retain those customers and expand their business with you over time.

Extensive research, across companies big and small, as to why customers leave shows some interesting results:

Reasons Why Customers Leave

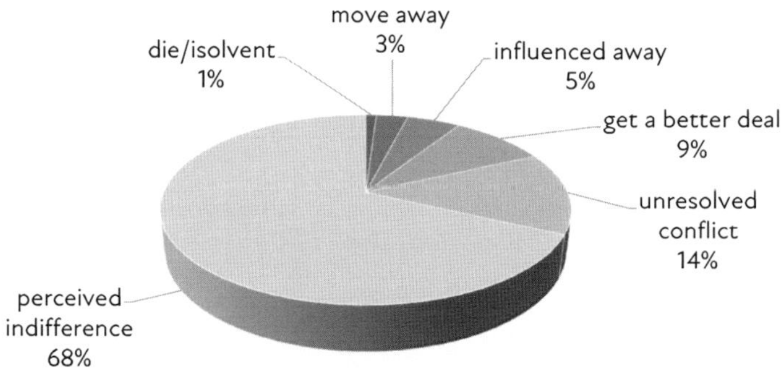

Read the findings of the study on why customers leave

Here is a great opportunity to avoid spending vast sums chasing new customers. Remember, many of the customers who leave used to love you!

If you can address the 82% who leave because of unresolved conflict and perceived indifference and aim to win back a good portion of them, your growth targets will become easier to achieve. Then, of course, you need to put in place the mechanisms to ensure that you won't lose them or other customers again.

I worked with a client who saw membership numbers steadily decline over a number of years. The CEO reported that they had spent significant amounts of effort and money on marketing initiatives, but still had a net drop in membership.

When I asked when last the organisation had done a member satisfaction survey, the answer was 'about three or four years ago'. And when I asked about the outcome and actions taken based on the survey results, the CEO said: 'We looked at them but then just filed them.' That is a huge opportunity missed!

We then ran a redesigned survey, and the results showed exactly what the client needed to improve to stop members from cancelling their subscriptions.

You've got to stop being afraid of letting your customers tell you why they left – or are considering leaving. Invite feedback, embrace it, and then do better.

Juanita

I was about to run a workshop for a group of CEOs, but before I started one of the members wanted to share something with me following a workshop I had run with them 18 months previously. He said: 'When you were here last time, you spoke about getting back lost customers, and it struck a chord with me. I realised that having put all that work into gaining customers, we didn't even track when we lost them. Back in the office, we got together a list of all customers lost in the past three years, and we approached them all – because, as you had said, they used to love us, why shouldn't they love us again? I have to tell you that as a result, in the last financial year 40% of our sales came from lost customers we got back. Thank you!'

Roger

The best antidote to perceived indifference is regular and varied communication at all levels. Classic wisdom is that your clients need to hear from you at least once every six weeks for them to not feel that you don't care about them. Sending existing customers information on special deals available to absolutely anyone does not count!

You might think that your marketing people have this under control – and you might be very wrong.

Ask your marketing team how often existing customers receive communication from the organisation and what the contents of that communication is. The answer very often reveals that more focus is placed on attracting new customers than on making existing customers feel valued.

Your customers also want to hear from you, the leader of the business:

- When did you, or your business, last genuinely say thank you to your customers?
- Do you share your long-term strategy with your customers?
- Do you involve them in your new product development?
- When did you last invite their CEO to dinner? (And not because you were after something specific.)

Regularly meet with your top customers – NOT to ask for an order.

There is ample opportunity to grow the profitability of your existing customers. In our masterclasses, we often ask CEOs:

'Do all your customers know about everything you do?'

We are amazed at how often we see shakes of the head!

Customer needs grow and change over time and your product offering changes – make sure your sales and marketing people keep all existing customers up to date with everything else you can do for them.

There are three simple metrics you should measure to grow the profitability of your existing customers. Although you'll rarely find these in any set of accounts or management information pack, they are very easy to establish for any business:

- number of customers
- average order value
- frequency of order placement

By setting and achieving modest growth targets for all three, you will readily achieve your overall sales growth aspirations. Don't believe us? Try this:

Let's say you have 2 000 customers who each, on average, buy three times per year, and their average order value is $10 000. Let's then set really modest growth targets – say 3% more customers, frequency in buying up just 10%, and a 3% increase in order value. Do the maths – the combination of those modest targets gives you sales growth of nearly 17%!

Increase Existing Customer Value

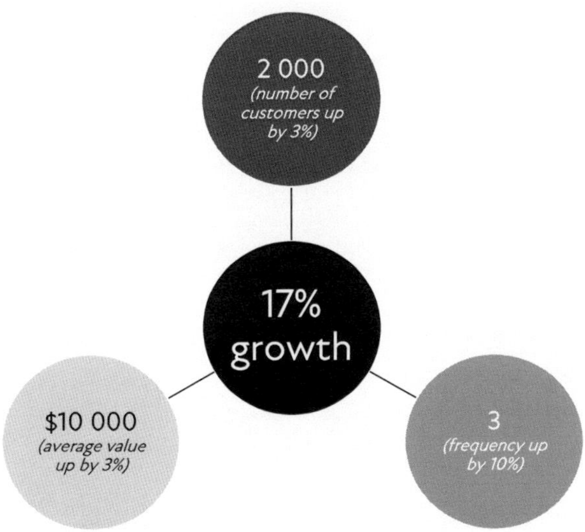

Of course, you can't do all of this alone. So next in our 'helicopter', we'll look at how to go about finding people who can help you.

THE PEOPLE

Finding top talent is not a job that can simply be delegated to HR.

WE ASKED BUSINESS leaders of companies large and small, for-profit and not-for-profit, what they believe the single biggest factor is that will inhibit profitable growth into the future.

Close to 40% of them responded that it was people. This means that recruitment has got to be worth you putting significant effort into.

Don't skip this section!

Most business leaders and managers prioritise other tasks over recruitment and selection, but we believe that you being personally involved is worth it – massively worth it. We see it as a vital part of your job to ensure that you get the right people for the right jobs throughout your organisation – even more so when you're managing a remote workforce.

Statistically, the success rate you'll achieve using the traditional method of interview-based recruitment is just two in five. That's a 60% failure rate! Is there anywhere else in your business where you would accept that degree of failure?

Our plea to every business leader is to get in your 'helicopter' and ask yourself: 'Can there be anything more important to the sustained profitable growth of my organisation than getting recruiting right?' Then, please invest enough of your time and finances to ensure that you seek to recruit right every time!

There are proven methodologies we use that will move your success rate up so that maybe four out of every five appointments are recruitment successes – but you will have to get personally involved.

We see getting the right people for the right jobs as a four-stage process with each step being of equal importance.

Four Stages of Recruitment

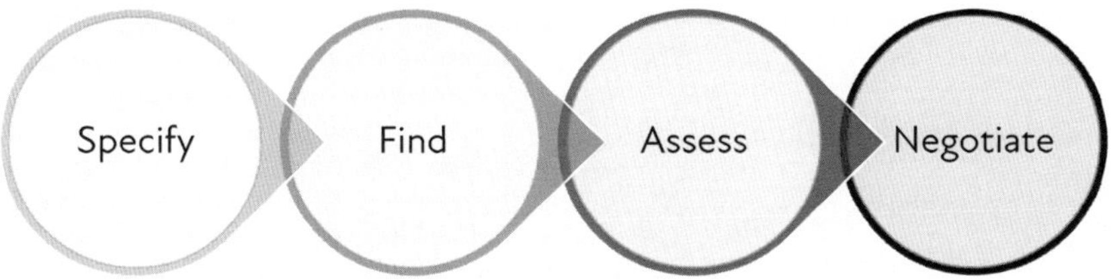

SPECIFY

Top talent isn't always looking for the highest-paying job with the biggest employer. The values and culture of an organisation increasingly play a bigger role in the job offers people accept.

So don't believe for a second that you have to settle for less than the best!

Before you start finding people, you need to be crystal clear about what you want. You must be clear about the job specification and the specification of the person you're looking for to fill it. This, in turn, needs to align with the purpose, vision, values and shape of the business. Please don't delegate this task to HR or your PA!

Never fall into the trap of thinking 'We'll decide what the details of the job are when we see who we can get.' This often leads to the actual specification being built around someone the interviewer likes instead of someone the organisation needs.

If we only recruit people we like or those that 'have the right chemistry', we run the risk of not only cloning ourselves but also not achieving that all-essential mix of behavioural competencies in our team. The only way to avoid these mistakes is to be very clear about what you want the ideal person to be able to do as well as the attitude and behaviours you want them to exhibit.

I worked with an ambitious small business owner with big expansion plans. He was, however, quite frustrated – his plan was sound, but things just didn't seem to come together.

After asking him a bunch of questions that varied from operations to industry trends to marketing activities, I realised that this owner was doing everything right – except for finding the right people.

The people he recruited to activate his expansion plan were very similar to himself – highly driven and ambitious. While they had the perfect chemistry and skills for the job, they always stayed only until they'd learned the ropes – and then moved on to start their own competing businesses!

Once the owner understood this, he started spending a lot more time and effort on creating a job and person specification that allowed him to find the people he needed to help build the business he wanted.

Juanita

Have a look at how Netflix describes their ideal employees

Netflix is well-known for using its culture as a competitive differentiator. On their website, the company makes it very clear which type of people will perform well.

The leadership style and people you employ for a business driven by operational excellence are likely to be quite different to one driven by product leadership and different again for an organisation driven by customer intimacy. Hence, the winning culture of each will differ.

Whatever the culture of your organisation and the technical job specifications, make sure that everything is clearly defined – and written down so it can be easily shared.

It may appear painfully obvious, but every so often we find that this has not been considered, or if it has been thought about it's not been written down clearly, which makes it difficult to keep an eye on the recruitment process.

FIND

You need to go into the process of finding candidates positively and with the clear intention of getting as many applications as possible.

You definitely don't just want to attract those who are looking to get away from their current employer – your ideal candidate might currently be happily employed but would also want an opportunity to work for you!

There are more ways of finding candidates for a job than ever before – social media, especially, has made it incredibly simple and often very cheap to spread the word about your job opening.

One of the things you need to do to maximise the number of candidates is to 'sell' your company and the job to them.

Your job advertisements should be much more than just a list of tasks and competencies.

Our advice is to have your marketing people prepare the job ad – they're experts in selling your company (unlike the HR department or even recruitment agencies). Make sure the job ad truly reflects the culture and values of the business and what it's like to be part of your team.

ASSESS

We continue to be amazed by just how many companies around the world still just use one or two interviews to recruit people and then talk about 'chemistry' or an impressive CV being the main factor in selecting a candidate.

I assisted a client with the recruitment and selection of a candidate for a key position in their marketing department. During the first recruitment round there were many applicants who seemed appropriately experienced until it came to assessing their skills – none could live up to the claims they made on their CVs.

After working with the client to clarify the job and person profile specification, I helped them create a new job ad to kickstart the second recruitment round. One of the candidates who had applied for the role in the first round applied again in the second round and listed that he had worked with my client on a project. His proof? The assessment he completed during the first recruitment round!

Don't believe everything you see on a CV or social media profile – test it for yourself!

Juanita

You can't rely simply on CVs and interviews to select the best candidate. You can't rely on references either – they are often of little value in these days of rising litigation. It is not unusual for lawyers to include in a termination agreement a clause committing the former employer to providing a good reference for the former employee.

If you were to recruit a chef, you'd ask them to prepare a meal for you, right? So why not ask a salesperson to prove that they can sell or an accountant that they can read, interpret and report on a set of accounts?

It is up to you to assess the candidates' skills and behavioural competencies.

We are great believers in using every possible tool to do that. These may appear to be time-consuming and costly, but it's much less expensive to use them than to recruit and train an employee who was never right for the job or whose aspirations conflicted with those of the business. The cost of getting it wrong has been estimated as about four or even five times the employee's annual salary.

The assessment process is so critical that it's worth putting a great deal of effort into getting it right. It could be a full one-day assessment centre run by a facilitator and incorporating group and individual activities for all short-listed candidates. You could also include – as a second level differentiator only – verbal, numerical and diagrammatic reasoning and a psychometric analysis.

No matter what the position, you should target a minimum of four and a maximum of six people to go through some type of detailed, objective, unbiased assessment process.

From our experience in selecting candidates for positions from shop floor supervisor to CEO, new graduates to seasoned professionals, we guess that in well over half of the cases the candidate who had been the favourite before the assessment phase was not the candidate who came through at the end as the right person for the job.

I was the new chairman of an engineering business selling hi-tech commodity products to original equipment manufacturers around the world. We were looking for a new Technical Director. I strongly recommended to my CEO that we use a one-day assessment centre process to select a candidate from the short list. He was very sceptical and said that he already knew who the successful candidate would be.

On my insistence, we went ahead with carefully crafted candidate group sessions and individual evaluations – with a good deal of time pressure put on the candidates.

My CEO was right – his chosen candidate was well ahead of the others in the morning. However, when it came to the afternoon he completely ran out of stamina and started making bad decisions.

I don't think we could have found that out any other way ahead of employing him – and finding out in the worst possible way.

Needless to say, my CEO was sold on this way of recruiting!

Roger

NEGOTIATE

The final stage in the recruitment process should be a face-to-face discussion and negotiation between the selected candidate and their 'boss to be'. We also recommend a period of probation before the job is finally confirmed and to have in place the legal documentation around this probation period.

Read about what employees want in our book WIN! How to Succeed in the New Game of Business

Once the probation period has been successfully completed, it's time to shift the focus to keeping the talent you worked so hard at getting. We have an entire chapter dedicated to retaining top talent in our book *WIN! How to Succeed in the New Game of Business*.

To ensure that these recruitment efforts continue to pay off, a organisation must be led by a leader that embraces the four dimensions of leadership – the next area of focus in our 'helicopter'.

THE LEADER

People will follow what you do, not what you say.

LEADERSHIP IS ONE of the greatest balancing acts. As a business leader, it is your responsibility to set and adjust the direction and pace according to what is happening in and around the business. Having your finger on the pulse of all the 'helicopter' areas of the business will allow you to run the business with both efficiency and empathy.

To lead with efficiency and empathy you need to continually hone the essential four dimensions of leadership.

Four-Dimensional Leadership

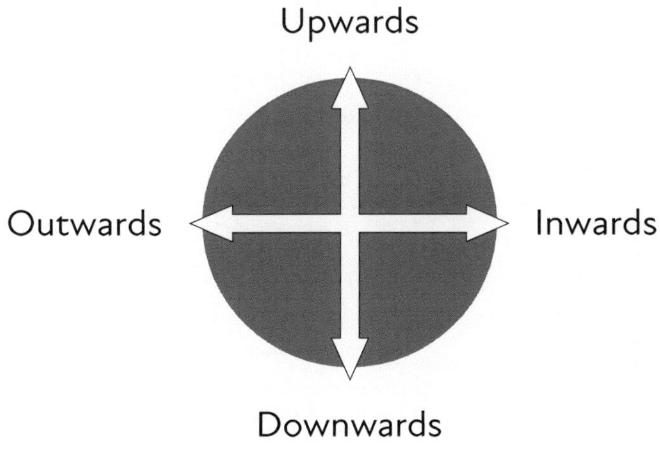

INWARDS LEADERSHIP

We first need to learn how to lead ourselves before we can effectively lead others.

Inwards leadership is all about taking responsibility for your own continued personal development. It's not enough for leaders to be highly proficient in their area of technical expertise – their ongoing leadership development must strike a good balance between technical skills and people skills.

Inwards leadership requires daily introspection to identify areas in which you might need to improve. The power of inwards leadership isn't knowing that you are imperfect but taking responsibility for your own improvement by acknowledging mistakes, saying sorry when you need to, and consistently working at changing your behaviour and improving your leadership skills.

Inwards leadership is also about doing the right thing even when no one is looking. This is especially important for those without formal governing structures to report to or those who are seen to be 'the big boss'.

Great leaders don't just do what they want: they know the rules, they know the reason for the rules, and they set an example for others on how to follow the rules.

In addition, great leaders know when and how to challenge the rules through upwards leadership.

UPWARDS LEADERSHIP

Upwards leadership is the dimension most often forgotten – and is probably the most difficult of the leadership dimensions. It is about having courage and telling those above you what they need to hear rather than what they may want to hear.

There are three laws of assertiveness in leading those above us:

- confront early

- if you want to say 'yes' say 'yes'
- if you want to say 'no' say 'no'

Too few business leaders do this for fear of losing their jobs or making life difficult for themselves – but this is part of your job!

When you're CEO of a company governed by a board or similar structure, you need to make sure that you don't just take instruction from the board but that you are actively involved in the decision-making process.

In the chapter 'The Real Objective', we discuss the essential need for an employed CEO to know the purpose of the organisation – this may well involve you exercising carefully planned upward leadership skills. Although this may prove very difficult, it's far too important to avoid.

If you're running a department or area, you must develop the skills you need to communicate upwards. You play an integral role in keeping top management aware of what is happening in and around the business – don't neglect this part of your responsibilities!

At the age of 32, I was appointed to run a company as managing director for the first time. My boss was in his 60s, and I'm sure that appointing me felt like a big risk for him. Unfortunately, he seemed to deal with that by visiting the company whenever I was out of the office for any reason and often changing instructions I had given and decisions we had made in the top team.

I was extremely concerned to confront him about this, but I just couldn't let it continue. I prepared in some detail: I instructed myself to stay in 'adult' mode – to avoid any emotion or histrionics – and to just stick with the facts and what I saw as the consequences of his actions.

It was amazing! He apologised and we agreed that we would both communicate more and always be straight with each other. From that moment on, he became one of the best bosses I ever had.

Roger

Upwards leadership is not about challenging the way things are for no specific reason. Upwards leadership is calm, composed, and considerate of why things are the way they are – while always striving to do better.

Great leaders don't make suggestions upwards to serve their own agenda but rather to ignite change for the greater good.

If you're both the owner and the leader of the business, we recommend that you surround yourself with people who are allowed to tell you what you need to – but might not want to – hear.

Leadership is a journey without an absolute top or bottom: we are all leading someone, whether we're aware of it or not. That means we have to pave the way upwards for those who follow in our footsteps.

It also means that we have to make it easy for those following us to tell us what we need to hear but might not want to hear. How easy do you make it for those below you to tell you what you need to hear?

DOWNWARDS LEADERSHIP

We find it fascinating that good leaders are often bad managers, and good managers are often bad leaders.

Leading with too much of the hard stuff often results in people feeling unappreciated and uninspired. On the other hand, leading with too much of the soft stuff can make for a happy but unproductive workplace or even massive corporate scandals.

You can't afford to say: 'This is my leadership style and I'm sticking to it!'

Downwards leadership is not just about what the leader wants from the team but what the team wants from the leader. All teams need direction, structure, organisation and motivation – and they want to be listened to. You have to make it easy for teams to talk to you, and you've got to listen attentively when they talk.

Great leaders don't need to know the details of everything in the business, but they must know how to get people and teams to do what they need to through a combination of inspiration, communication, trust and discipline. The following questions can guide you in this:

- When last did you tell your people where you're going and why you're going there?
- When last did you make sure that everyone knows what role they play in the bigger picture of the business?
- Do you have checks and balances in place to track performance without micromanaging people?
- Do you discipline those who step out of line quickly and appropriately?

OUTWARDS LEADERSHIP

Business leaders have a great opportunity to shape the industry in which their organisations operate. As our world becomes increasingly interconnected, great leaders know that they can't just protect their own followers – they've got to play an active role in making the world a better place and setting others up for success.

Outwards leadership is about influencing systems outside your business to make it easier for an entire industry to operate efficiently.

Great leaders don't bunker down in gilded offices: they walk the talk, participate in industry discussions, and become involved in causes aligned with the business purpose.

We've seen outwards leadership trigger industry-wide regulation change, increase transparency and fair competition, standardise quality, and even shine a welcome spotlight on corrupt 'everybody-does-it' ways of doing business.

Don't be scared to do this! Yes, your competitors might benefit in some way, but the unique set of 'helicopter' skills you have now acquired far outweigh that benefit.

All leaders of all businesses of all sizes and shapes must keep working on developing attitudes that genuinely inspire others to follow them. Looking down from our helicopter, it is clear that the successful leader needs to exhibit three qualities above all others: belief, passion and courage.

Great leaders know where they're going and why, and they **believe** 100% in that vision. The strength of their belief is like a magnet, and others can't help but get excited about aligning themselves with that vision.

Great leaders exhibit authentic **passion** for the business and their responsibilities, and they have clear values that set the tone for everyone who follows them.

Great leaders have the **courage** to make the really difficult decisions, take risks, and deal with the consequences.

You have to lead with vitality and energy – especially in times of crisis or change, which is what we look at next from our 'helicopter'.

THE FUTURE

'We've always done it this way' is the beginning of the end.

TECHNOLOGICAL ADVANCES (AND global pandemics!) aren't the only reasons a business leader should have the skill to lead during times of change. Shifts in what society demands of business, where markets emerge, and even short-lived fashionable trends all force organisations to be in a constant state of renewal.

Getting to a state of constant – and willing – renewal depends on how well the business leader manages change throughout the organisation.

The Change House is our favourite model of organisational change. It proposes that any organisation, department, team or even individual exists at any time in one of four 'rooms' and can only move from room to room in a predetermined sequence. The leadership needs of the business (and the people in it) are different for each room.

Many of our clients, delegates and readers have told us how valuable they find this model as a tool in their 'helicopter' kit.

The Change House Model

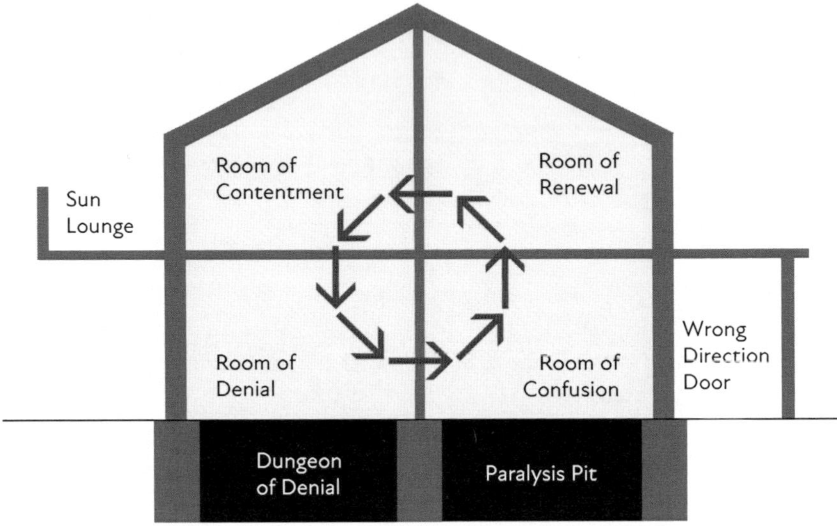

The Change House Model© is used with permission of The Change House Limited

ROOM OF CONTENTMENT

Here you will find organisations, teams, groups and individuals that may have been highly successful – and possibly still are – but have allowed themselves the luxury of thinking that they know it all. They believe if they carry on the way they always have, they will be – and are indeed entitled to be – continually successful.

The culture is one of: 'We know exactly what we're doing: we've been the market leader for the last 10 years and our business model is the ONLY business model.' That's where Coca-Cola was when Red Bull arrived. That's where Microsoft was when Google started as an internet search engine. That's where Caterpillar was when Komatsu arrived. That's where – in our experience – government-owned organisations have difficulty not being.

In the mid-2000s, Marks & Spencer in the UK were out on the sun lounge. Their approach: 'It's just so easy making money! We will never offer credit cards. We will never be at motorway service stations.'

Prior to the COVID-19 pandemic, we saw many companies in the retail space firmly stuck in the room of contentment whilst, in reality, the traditional retail business model was under massive threat from online sales.

Organisations in the room of contentment are characterised by a tendency towards smugness, complacency, arrogance and conceit. The immediate signs to look for include lots of self-praising internal publications and recruitment processes that favour 'people like us'.

There is only one place to go from here.

ROOM OF DENIAL

You'll find a lot of finger-pointing in this room – any problems are 'transient' or 'someone else's fault'. It's the recession, the pandemic, the market sector, the exchange rate, the government, the weather... it's anyone but us. There's a focus on looking to past achievements, while people become irrationally optimistic and search for comforting data – and, of course, people make statements like: 'Our business is different'.

If you're in the room of denial, you need some sort of catalyst to get you out – otherwise you end up in the dungeon of denial. In the dungeon of denial, even though the receivers are circling, you still say: 'Oh, don't worry! It's just temporary, it's just a blip.'

The catalyst for change in a large organisation is often a new CEO and usually a shaper (according to the Belbin profiles we discuss in our book *WIN! How to Succeed in the New Game of Business*).

The catalyst for change is someone who comes in and says: 'That's where we're going, follow me!' In a smaller organisation you need wholly objective, unsentimental advice – and you won't get that from colleagues, family or friends. You are most likely to get that from an outsider like an independent director, an adviser, or a peer group. You need somebody to say: 'Look, I think you're in denial, and you need to do something about it!'

Assuming you do something to move out of the room of denial, your next destination is the room of confusion.

ROOM OF CONFUSION

This is where things are done half the old way and half the new way, and it's all very confusing for everybody. There's a steady stream of new people coming and experienced people going and rumours swirling around.

One of the dangers in the room of confusion is that employees might say to themselves: 'We've been going in a certain direction for years and now we're being told to go in a different direction – the safest thing we can do is to keep our heads down until it all blows over.' This means that they're in the paralysis pit and can cause the whole place to seize up.

Another danger here is going through the wrong direction door. As the room of confusion is so uncomfortable, this door is sometimes seen as a bit of relief: people dash through it in an ill-thought-out direction that solves nothing.

To survive this room and move into the next, it's vital that the leader continues to repeat the simple message and goal set in the room of denial, as it functions as the light at the end of the tunnel.

Watch an animation of The Change House

ROOM OF RENEWAL

You need to get to the room of renewal. This is where you challenge every paradigm in the business. It's where absolutely nothing you do is done simply because you've always done it that way. You look at everything in the business and ask yourself if it's right for the future – if the answer is 'no', you change it or get rid of it.

Even if it's the crown jewels that the business was built on: if it isn't right for the business tomorrow, it has to go.

The room of renewal is the only safe room to be in. Here your organisation is robust and prepared for almost anything. In this room, there are no signs of complacency or resting on laurels. It's also where you're always raising the bar and saying: 'We can do better!'

Here you find everyone singing the same tune, taking ownership, and working together. Problems are seen as 'ours', progress is measured, and new targets are set. While success is celebrated, the paradigms are constantly challenged.

The single most important focus for any organisation is probably to work out how to not just get into the room of renewal but also how to stay there! It is much harder than you think, which makes the room of contentment so very alluring.

YOUR FLIGHT PLAN

Don't just put this book on the shelf!

To be effective in your 'helicopter', you've got to become good at talking and listening to yourself.

These days – more than ever before – you've got to spend at least 20% of your time in the 'helicopter' looking at the big picture. That's a day a week.

We know you don't have time to spare. We know your heart says you should do something about what you've read in this book, but your head says you're too busy. Thinking about what you've read, can you really afford to not take these simple steps towards sustained profitable growth?

So, how do you find that elusive 20% of your time?

Set yourself a realistic programme right now.

Promise yourself that you'll get in your helicopter at least once a month. Start by putting the next six occasions firmly in your diary. Address a section of this book each time and put specific actions in place.

You've got to trust people and delegate more.

Never mind how young or inexperienced they are, don't micromanage your staff. Try it! You might just be pleasantly surprised by how well it works out.

Don't let yourself get sucked into the details.

If you have a task to be done, give it to the team. Tell them to evaluate it and come up with a proposed action and alternatives by a certain time. Now, stand back and observe. You'll be amazed by what you see and the clarity they find when they take ownership of the task.

Have a look at your business from the 'helicopter' and see what you believe you can achieve. Now, go out and make it happen!

Remember, the only way to complete a journey is to take it one step – or 'helicopter flight' – at a time.

Good luck and enjoy the journey!

STAY IN TOUCH WITH US

Roger Harrop
roger@rogerharrop.com
www.rogerharrop.com

Juanita Vorster
juanita@juanitavorster.com
www.juanitavorster.com

Book us for keynote speeches and masterclasses on these topics, each tailored to your needs and ideal outcomes:

- Staying in the Helicopter®: The Key to Sustained Profitable Growth
- WIN! How to Succeed in the New Game of Business
- Electrify Your Profitability™
- Sparkling Sales – In Good Times or Bad
- Effective Leadership Today
- Creativity, Technology, Speed and Change
- Present & Pitch for Profit

www.theceoexperts.com